TRUSTING IN CHRIST

JESUS CALLING BIBLE STUDY SERIES

TRUSTING IN CHRIST

EIGHT SESSIONS

Sarah Young

with Karen Lee-Thorp

THOMAS NELSON
Since 1798

NASHVILLE   MEXICO CITY   RIO DE JANEIRO

Published in Nashville, Tennessee, by Nelson Books, an imprint of Thomas Nelson. Nelson Books and Thomas Nelson are registered trademarks of HarperCollins Christian Publishing, Inc.

All Scripture quotations, unless otherwise indicated, are taken from The Holy Bible, *New International Version*®, NIV®. Copyright © 1973, 1978, 1984, 2011 by Biblica, Inc.® Used by permission. All rights reserved worldwide.

Scripture quotations marked ESV are taken from *The Holy Bible, English Standard Version,* copyright © 2001 by Crossway Bibles, a division of Good News Publishers. Used by permission. All rights reserved.

Scripture quotations marked NKJV are taken from the New King James Version. Copyright © 1982 by Thomas Nelson, Inc. Used by permission. All rights reserved.

ISBN 978-0-7180-3587-7

First Printing May 2015 / Printed in the United States of America

CONTENTS

INTRODUCTION

Sometimes our busy and difficult lives give us the impression that God is silent. We cry out to Him, but our feelings tell us that He isn't answering our prayers. In this, our feelings are incorrect. God hears our prayers and speaks right into the situations in which we find ourselves. The trouble is that our lives are often too hectic, our minds too distracted, for us to take in what God offers.

This *Jesus Calling* Bible study is designed to help individuals and groups meditate on the words of Scripture and hear them not just as words said to people long ago but as words said to us today in the here and now. The goal is to help the heart hear and respond to what the mind reads—to encounter the living God as He speaks through the Scriptures. The writer to the Hebrews tells us:

In the past God spoke to our ancestors through the prophets at many times and in various ways, but in these last days he has spoken to us by his Son, whom he appointed heir of all things, and through whom also he made the universe. The Son is the radiance of God's glory and the exact representation of his being, sustaining all things by his powerful word.

—HEBREWS 1:1–3

God has spoken to us through His Son, Jesus Christ. The New Testament gives us the chance to walk with Jesus, see what He does, and hear Him speak into the sometimes confusing situations in which we find ourselves. The Old Testament tells us the story of how God prepared a people to be the family of Jesus, and in the experiences of those men and women we find our own lives mirrored.

THE GOAL OF THIS SERIES

The *Jesus Calling Bible Study Series* offers you a chance to lay down your cares, enter God's Presence, and hear Him speak through His Word. You will get to spend some time in silence studying a passage of Scripture, and then if you're meeting with a group, share your insights and hear what others discovered. You'll also get to discuss excerpts from the *Jesus Calling* devotional that relate to the themes of the Bible passages. In this way, you will learn how to better make space in your life for the Spirit of God to speak to you through the Word of God and the people of God.

THE FLOW OF EACH SESSION

Each session of this study guide contains the following elements:

- CONSIDER IT. The one or two questions in this opening section serve as an icebreaker to help you start to think about the theme of the session. These questions will help you connect the theme to your own past or present experience and will help you get to know the others in your group more deeply. If you've had a busy day and your mind is full of distractions, this section will help you better focus.

- EXPERIENCE IT. Here you will find two readings from *Jesus Calling,* along with some questions for reflection. This is your chance to talk with others about the biblical principles found within the *Jesus Calling* devotions. Can you relate to what each reading describes? What insights from God's Word does it illuminate? What does it motivate you to do? This section will help you apply these biblical principles to your everyday habits.

- STUDY IT. Next, you'll explore one or two Scripture passages connected to the session topic and the readings from *Jesus Calling.* You will not only analyze these passages but also pray through them in ways designed to engage your heart as well as your head. In some cases the passage will be a biblical story, and you'll spend five to ten minutes in silence imagining what it was like to be there in that moment. If you're meeting with a group, you will then talk about what you learned and how the passage is relevant to your life. In other cases, the passage will be a teaching from Jesus or the apostle Paul. You'll first talk with your group about what the passage means and then spend several minutes in silence, letting God speak into your life through His Word.

- LIVE IT. Finally, you will find five days' worth of suggested Scripture passages that you can pray through on your own during the week. Suggested questions for additional study and reflection are provided.

During the *Study It* portion, you will want to make notes of what comes to mind when you imagine the scene in the Scripture passage. Be sure to bring a pen to record your thoughts. The Bible passage itself is provided for you in this study guide.

FOR LEADERS

If you are leading a group through this study guide, please see the Leader's Notes at the end of the guide. You'll find background on the design of the study as well as suggested answers for some of the study questions.

TRUSTING IN GOD'S STRENGTH

CONSIDER IT

So much of ordinary life is based on trust. When you climb out of bed in the morning, you trust the floor will support you so you can stand upright. When you go to the coffee house, you trust the people there will safely supply the ingredients for your breakfast. When you step into an elevator, you trust the maintenance crews have done what is necessary to make sure you won't get stuck between floors. If any of these betray your trust, it can be very disturbing.

Unfortunately, no structure, person, or human institution is perfectly trustworthy. Buildings wear out and fail. Food and water can be tainted. Maintenance crews miss things or fail to follow proper procedures. Even family and friends sometimes fail us. Our awareness of these flaws in people and things can leave us feeling insecure, as if there is no one or no thing we can truly trust.

The Bible claims God is different. He is *perfectly trustworthy*. This seems too good to be true, so we doubt it *is* true. Even when we want to trust what the Bible says about God, a lifetime of being let down by others leaves a core of mistrust inside us. We find it hard to believe God is all-powerful and can handle any situation that confronts us.

In this first session, we're going to become aware of that mistrust and whether we have a little of it or a lot. We're going to start chopping away at its roots so we can start to build trust in the One who can always be trusted.

1. *On a scale of 1 to 5, how would you rate your ability on a typical day to relax and trust in God's strength?*

1	2	3	4	5
I find it hard to trust God.			I find it easy to trust God.	

2. *What about today? What helped you trust God? What got in the way?*

EXPERIENCE IT

"Strive to trust Me in more and more areas of your life. Anything that tends to make you anxious is a growth opportunity. Instead of running away from these challenges, embrace them, eager to gain all the blessings I have hidden in the difficulties. If you believe that I am sovereign over every aspect of your life, it is possible to trust Me in all situations. Don't waste energy regretting the way things are or thinking about what might have been. Start at the present moment—accepting things exactly as they are—and search for My way in the midst of those circumstances.

"Trust is like a staff you can lean on, as you journey uphill with Me. If you are trusting in Me consistently, the staff will bear as much of your weight as needed. *Lean on, trust, and be confident in Me with all your heart and mind.*"

—FROM *JESUS CALLING*, JANUARY 22

3. *Do you have a tendency to get anxious? If so, what sorts of things do you get anxious about? Why do you worry?*

_____

_____

_____

_____

4. *What do you see in the above reading that is different from your typical approach to the things that make you anxious?*

_____

_____

_____

_____

5. *What appeals to you in what you see there? Does anything not appeal? Why?*

_____

_____

_____

_____

"I want you to learn a new habit. Try saying, 'I trust You, Jesus,' in response to whatever happens to you. If there is time, think about who I am in all My Power and Glory; ponder also the depth and breadth of My Love for you.

"This simple practice will help you see Me in every situation, acknowledging My sovereign control over the universe. When you view events from this perspective—through the Light of My universal Presence—fear loses its grip on you. Adverse circumstances become growth opportunities when you affirm your trust in Me no matter what. You receive blessings gratefully, realizing they flow directly from My hand of grace. Your continual assertion of trusting Me will strengthen our relationship and keep you close to Me."

—FROM *JESUS CALLING*, JANUARY 4

6. *What do you think of the idea of saying, "I trust You, Jesus," in response to everything that happens? Do you think that would help you? What obstacles would you have to overcome to make that a habit?*

_____

_____

_____

_____

7. *What would be some benefits of praying this consistently? Which benefits seem especially significant to you? Why?*

STUDY IT

Read aloud the following passage from Matthew 6:25–34. Jesus speaks these words to His followers. Try to hear Him speaking them to you.

"Therefore I tell you, do not worry about your life, what you will eat or drink; or about your body, what you will wear. Is not life more than food, and the body more than clothes? Look at the birds of the air; they do not sow or reap or store away in barns, and yet your heavenly Father feeds them. Are you not much more valuable than they? Can any one of you by worrying add a single hour to your life?

"And why do you worry about clothes? See how the flowers of the field grow. They do not labor or spin. Yet I tell you that not even Solomon in all his splendor was dressed like one of these. If that is how God clothes the grass of the field, which is here today and tomorrow is thrown into the fire, will he not much more clothe you—you of little faith? So do not worry, saying, 'What shall we eat?' or 'What shall we drink?' or 'What shall we wear?' For the pagans run after all these things, and your heavenly Father knows that you need them. But seek first his kingdom and his righteousness, and all these things will be given to you as well. Therefore do not worry about tomorrow, for tomorrow will worry about itself. Each day has enough trouble of its own."

8. *In the passage above, what reasons does Jesus give for not worrying? List as many as you can.*

9. *Which of these reasons do you find persuasive? Why? Which ones are more difficult to accept?*

10. *Take two minutes of silence to reread the passage, looking for a sentence, phrase, or even one word that stands out as something Jesus wants you to hear. Ask Him to help you hear it. If you're meeting with a group, the leader will keep track of time. At the end of two minutes, you may share your word or phrase with the group if you wish.*

11. *Read the passage aloud again. Take two minutes of silence, asking Jesus what He is saying to you through the word or phrase you selected, and whether He would like you to do anything in response. If you're meeting with a group, the leader will again keep track of time. At the end of two minutes, you may share with the group what came to you in the silence if you wish.*

12. *What was it like for you to sit in silence with the passage? Did soaking in the passage like this help you take it in better than before?*

13. *If you're meeting with a group, how can the members pray for you? If you're using this study on your own, what would you like to say to God right now?*

LIVE IT

At the end of each session you'll find suggested Scripture readings for spending time alone with God during five days of the coming week. Each day will deal with this week's theme of letting go of worry and trusting in God's strength. Read the passage slowly, pausing to think about what is being said. Rather than approaching this as an assignment to complete, think of it as an opportunity to meet with a Person. Use any of the questions that are helpful.

Day 1

Read Proverbs 3:5–6. Why is it unwise to rely on your own understanding? Give an example of a way in which your understanding is limited.

What path are you currently most concerned about?

Are you tempted to worry about it? How could leaning on the Lord's strength help you?

_____

_____

_____

_____

What would acknowledging Him in that situation look like?

_____

_____

_____

_____

Pray aloud, "I trust you, Jesus."

Day 2

Read Psalm 37:1–7. What does it mean to fret?

_____

_____

_____

_____

What causes of fretting does this psalm address?

_____

_____

_____

Do you ever fret for these reasons? What reasons does this psalm give for why you shouldn't fret?

_____

_____

_____

What promise do you most need to take to heart? How can you choose to take delight in the Lord today?

_____

_____

_____

Pray aloud, "I trust You, Jesus." Try to pray this several times during the coming day.

Day 3

Read Isaiah 40:10–11. Think about the Lord coming with power. How has He displayed His power in the past?

_____

_____

_____

How does God display it in the world around you? How has He displayed it in your own life?

_____

_____

_____

How does God's power make Him trustworthy? How does thinking about it affect your anxiety?

_____

_____

_____

Ask God to give you a glimpse of His power. Pray aloud, "I trust You, Jesus." See if you can remember to pray it again throughout your day.

Day 4

Read Psalm 23:1–4. Stop at the end of each line and picture yourself in the scene, lying down in a green pasture, with a restored soul, and so on. What does it feel like?

_____

_____

_____

_____

Can you let your body relax into the scene? Can you picture yourself walking in the valley, comforted and strengthened rather than afraid? How does this psalm affect the way you see the situations you are tempted to worry about?

_____

_____

_____

_____

Pray aloud right now, "I trust You, Jesus," and do so continually as you go through your day. Pray to be aware of Jesus' Presence and strength.

Day 5

Read Psalm 127:1–2. What does it mean to trust the Lord to build your house? Do you think He will?

Do you think God is powerful enough to keep your town safe? Do you think that He will do so?

What are the worries that threaten your sleep?

Why is anxious toil unnecessary? How is it different from hard work without anxiety?

_____

_____

_____

_____

Turn these verses into a prayer, entrusting to God the things that you tend to worry about. Pray aloud, "I trust You, Jesus."

TRUSTING IN
GOD'S GOODNESS

CONSIDER IT

How do you imagine God when you pray? Is He listening with rapt attention and a smile on His face? Is He frowning at a pile of paperwork on His desk, hardly noticing you're talking? Is He engrossed listening to someone else—someone more deserving?

Whatever your notion of God, it influences the way you pray. It influences what you ask for, how persistently you ask if He doesn't answer right away, and whether you trust Him to hear you and have your best interests at heart.

In this session you'll read a parable in which Jesus gets at the way each of us imagines God. As you study that story, it will challenge the way you see God and approach Him in prayer.

1. *In session 1, you were challenged to pray, "I trust You, Jesus," as you went through your day. Did you try it? If so, how did it affect your attitude and actions? What was a high point or low point of your trust in God this week?*

EXPERIENCE IT

"I am able to do far beyond all that you ask or imagine. Come to Me with positive expectations, knowing that there is no limit to what I can accomplish. Ask My Spirit to control your mind, so that you can think great thoughts of Me. Do not be discouraged by the fact that many of your prayers are yet unanswered. Time is a trainer, teaching you to wait upon Me, to trust Me in the dark. The more extreme your circumstances, the more likely you are to see *My Power and Glory* at work in the situation. Instead of letting difficulties draw you into worrying, try

to view them as setting the scene for My glorious intervention. Keep your eyes and your mind wide open to all that I am doing in your life."

—From *Jesus Calling*, January 6

2. *Do you tend to get discouraged when your prayers are unanswered? Why or why not?*

_____

_____

_____

_____

3. *What reasons do we have for trusting God while we wait for an answer? Which ones seem especially motivating to you?*

_____

_____

_____

_____

"Do not resist or run from the difficulties in your life. These problems are not random mistakes; they are hand-tailored blessings designed for your benefit and growth. Embrace all the circumstances that I allow in your life, trusting Me to bring good out of them. View problems as opportunities to rely more fully on Me.

"When you start to feel stressed, let those feelings alert you to your need for Me. Thus, your needs become doorways to deep dependence on Me and increasing intimacy between us. Although self-sufficiency is acclaimed in the world, reliance on Me produces abundant living in My kingdom. Thank Me for the difficulties in your life, since they provide protection from the idolatry of self-reliance."

—FROM *JESUS CALLING*, MAY 10

4. *Think of a difficulty in your life. How could it encourage you to depend more on God? What would that dependence look like?*

_____

_____

_____

5. *Do you trust God enough to depend on Him in that situation? What encourages you to trust Him? What, if anything, discourages you?*

_____

_____

_____

_____

STUDY IT

Read aloud the following passage from Luke 18:1–8. Jesus speaks these words to His followers. Try to hear Him speaking them to you.

Then Jesus told his disciples a parable to show them that they should always pray and not give up. He said: "In a certain town there was a judge who neither feared God nor cared what people thought. And there was a widow in that town who kept coming to him with the plea, 'Grant me justice against my adversary.'

"For some time he refused. But finally he said to himself, 'Even though I don't fear God or care what people think, yet because this widow keeps bothering me, I will see that she gets justice, so that she won't eventually come and attack me!'"

And the Lord said, "Listen to what the unjust judge says. And will not God bring about justice for his chosen ones, who cry out to him day and night? Will he keep putting them off? I tell you, he will see that they get justice, and quickly. However, when the Son of Man comes, will he find faith on the earth?"

6. *Describe the judge in Jesus' story. What do you imagine he looks like? What tone of voice does he use when he speaks? What is his attitude toward the widow?*

7. *How is this judge like God? How is he different from God?*

8. *What lesson does Jesus draw from the story of the judge and the widow?*

_____

_____

_____

_____

9. *What is Jesus' point in comparing God to this judge? How does Jesus use this story to get at the way we tend to imagine God?*

_____

_____

_____

_____

10. *How are you like or unlike the widow in this story?*

_____

_____

_____

_____

11. *Take two minutes of silence to reread the passage, looking for a sentence, phrase, or even one word that stands out as something Jesus wants you to hear. Ask Him to help you hear it. If you're meeting with a group, the leader will keep track of time. At the end of two minutes, you may share your word or phrase with the group if you wish.*

---

12. *Read the passage aloud again. Take two minutes of silence, asking Jesus what He is saying to you through the word or phrase and whether He would like you to do anything in response. If you're meeting with a group, the leader will again keep track of time. At the end of two minutes, you may share with the group what came to you in the silence if you wish.*

---

13. *If you're meeting with a group, how can the members pray for you? If you're using this study on your own, what would you like to say to God right now?*

LIVE IT

The theme of this week's readings is trusting in the goodness of God and taking your needs to Him in prayer. Each day, read the passage slowly, pausing to think about what is being said. Rather than approaching this as an assignment to complete, think of it as an opportunity to meet with a Person. Use any of the questions that are helpful.

Day 1

Read Luke 18:9–14. What do you notice about the body language of the two characters in this story? What do the Pharisee's words and body language say about the focus of his trust? What do the tax collector's words and body language say about the focus of his trust?

How do you think each of them imagines God's character?

How does the Pharisee's trust affect the results of his prayer? How does the tax collector's trust affect the results of his prayer?

How is this story relevant to your own prayers?

What do you want to say to God right now?

_____

_____

_____

_____

Day 2

Read Psalm 61. What does this psalmist ask for in prayer? How does he express his trust in God?

_____

_____

_____

_____

Can you affirm any of his statements of trust, or do you question whether these things are true in your case?

_____

_____

_____

_____

What would you like to ask God for today?

Turn this psalm into a model for how you make requests and express trust in God.

Day 3

Read Psalm 6. What does this psalmist ask for? How does he express his trust in God?

How would you describe his emotions? Do those emotions fit with trust? Why or why not?

What emotions would you like to take to God in prayer today?

_____

_____

_____

_____

_____

Do so now and offer your prayer to God.

Day 4

Read Psalm 10:12–18. What does the psalmist pray for? How does he see God?

_____

_____

_____

_____

Can you identify with his words? If so, how?

_____

_____

_____

_____

Imagine the persistent widow from Jesus' story in Luke 18:1–8 praying this same prayer day after day. How long would it take to get tired of praying this? What would you do if you had to pray this for months before getting a response from God?

_____

_____

_____

_____

_____

Take the desires of your heart to God yet again. Tell Him you trust Him.

Day 5

Read Psalm 18:1–6. How is this prayer different from the ones in Psalms 6 and 10?

_____

_____

_____

_____

_____

How would you describe the psalmist's emotions here? How does he express trust in God?

_____

_____

_____

_____

What can you take from this passage and incorporate into a prayer to God today, even if you don't yet have the thing you are praying for?

_____

_____

_____

_____

TRUSTING IN GOD'S PRESENCE

CONSIDER IT

It's easy to feel God's Presence when life is going well. The test of our trust comes when something painful happens. When life is more difficult than we can manage, it's natural to wonder if God is really present and taking care of us. Some of us respond by worrying. Some of us respond by doubling down on our efforts to manage life on our own. Neither response embodies the dependence on God that He invites us to have. In this session we'll look at what helped the apostle Paul rely on God in the midst of his serious suffering.

1. *How would you rate the difficulty and suffering (physical or emotional) you're enduring at the moment?*

1	2	3	4	5	6	7	8	9	10

No suffering.   Worst suffering I can imagine.

2. *What is so difficult about that situation? Can you sense God's presence in it? Why or why not?*

EXPERIENCE IT

"Approach problems with a light touch. When your mind moves toward a problem area, you tend to focus on that situation so intensely that you lose sight of Me. You pit yourself against the difficulty as if you had to conquer it immediately. Your mind gears up for battle, and your body becomes tense and anxious. Unless you achieve total victory, you feel defeated.

"There is a better way. When a problem starts to overshadow your thoughts, bring this matter to Me. Talk with Me about it and look at it in the Light of My Presence. This puts some much-needed space between you and your concern, enabling you to see from My perspective. You will be surprised at the results. Sometimes you may even laugh at yourself for being so serious about something so insignificant.

"You will always face trouble in this life. But more importantly, you will always have Me with you, helping you to handle whatever you encounter. Approach problems with a light touch by viewing them in My revealing Light."

—FROM *JESUS CALLING*, NOVEMBER 15

3. *Do you tend to lose sight of Jesus when you are thinking about a problem? If so, how does that affect what you feel and what you do? If not, how do you stay focused on Jesus during those times?*

_____

_____

_____

_____

4. *What would it take for you to develop a habit of taking problems to Jesus? What would help you do that?*

_____

_____

_____

_____

"I am with you and for you. You face nothing alone—*nothing*! When you feel anxious, know that you are focusing on the visible world and leaving Me out of the picture. The remedy is simple: *Fix your eyes not on what is seen but on what is unseen.* Verbalize your trust in Me, *the Living One who sees you always.* I will get you safely through this day and all your days. But you can find Me only in the present. Each day is a precious gift from My Father. How ridiculous to grasp for future gifts when today's is set before you! Receive today's gift gratefully, unwrapping it tenderly and delving into its depths. As you savor this gift, you find Me."

—FROM *JESUS CALLING*, FEBRUARY 3

5. *What is the "unseen reality" on which Christians need to fix their eyes? Describe it as richly as you can.*

_____

_____

_____

_____

6. *How easy is it for you to "receive today's gift gratefully"—or, as the Bible says, "rejoice in it"—even when things are difficult? What helps you?*

_____

_____

_____

_____

STUDY IT

Read aloud the following passage from 2 Corinthians 4:6–12, 16–18. The apostle Paul is writing to his readers about how he deals with the severe challenges he is facing. He has been under cruel pressure from people who want to shut down his ministry, and his life has even been in danger (see 2 Corinthians 1:8–9).

> For God, who said, "Let light shine out of darkness," made his light shine in our hearts to give us the light of the knowledge of God's glory displayed in the face of Christ.
>
> But we have this treasure in jars of clay to show that this all-surpassing power is from God and not from us. We are hard pressed on every side, but not crushed; perplexed, but not in despair; persecuted, but not abandoned; struck down, but not destroyed. We always carry around in our body the death of Jesus, so that the life of Jesus may also be revealed in our body. For we who are alive are always being given over to death for Jesus' sake, so that his life may also be revealed in our mortal body. So then, death is at work in us, but life is at work in you . . .
>
> Therefore we do not lose heart. Though outwardly we are wasting away, yet inwardly we are being renewed day by day. For our light and momentary troubles are achieving for us an eternal glory that far outweighs them all. So we fix our eyes not on what is seen, but on what is unseen, since what is seen is temporary, but what is unseen is eternal.

Paul's secret to dealing with challenges is that he relies on "the light of the knowledge of God's glory" (verse 6). For Paul, the knowledge of God's glory isn't mere information about God but a deeper understanding of Him gained through personal experience. Paul experienced God's glorious Presence when he met the risen Christ on the road to Damascus (see Acts 9:1–9), and from that moment on no amount of suffering could detract him from the joy of sharing the light of Christ with others. Paul carries this knowledge-by-experience within him as he goes through his day.

7. *Has God given you "the knowledge of God's glory" as something you know by experience? If so, what difference has it made in your life? (Note: The experience of God's glorious Presence often isn't dramatic. It can be quiet and not obvious to other people.)*

---

8. *In the second paragraph of the reading, Paul speaks of "treasure in jars of clay." What is that treasure? What are the jars of clay? What point is Paul making in this sentence?*

---

9. *Because Paul has this treasure, he is "hard pressed . . . but not crushed," which means that his experiential knowledge of God's glorious Presence makes all the difference in the way his problems affect him. How does he describe his problems in the second and third paragraphs?*

---

10. *Take a moment to ask God to give you experiential knowledge of His glorious Presence. Read the passage aloud again and take three minutes of silence to sit with the passage, looking for a sentence, phrase, or even one word that stands out as something God wants you to hear. Ask Him to help you hear it and to help you know that He is right there with you, communicating through His Word. If you're meeting with a group, the leader will keep track of time. At the end of three minutes, share your word or phrase with the group if you wish.*

11. *Read the passage aloud again. Take three minutes of silence, asking God what He is saying to you and whether He would like you to do something in response. If you're meeting with a group, the leader will again keep track of time. At the end of three minutes, you may share with the group what came to you in the silence if you wish.*

12. *What was it like for you to sit in silence with this passage?*

13. *If you're meeting with a group, how can the members pray for you? If you're using this study on your own, what would you like to say to God right now?*

LIVE IT

The theme of this week's readings is trusting God is with you when things are difficult. Each day, read the passage slowly, pausing to think about what is being said. Rather than approaching this as an assignment to complete, think of it as an opportunity to meet with a Person. Use any of the questions that are helpful.

Day 1

Read 2 Corinthians 1:8–11. How serious is Paul's suffering? How does he describe it?

_____

_____

_____

_____

What purpose does he see in his suffering?

_____

_____

_____

_____

Does knowing that God raised Jesus from the dead increase your confidence in God? Why or why not?

_____

_____

_____

_____

How did prayer help Paul? Who could you ask to pray for you?

Ask God to help you rely on His Presence and trust Him as the One who is powerful enough to raise the dead.

Day 2

Read Psalm 27:1–5. What does it mean to call the Lord "my light" (verse 1)?

What does it mean to call him "the stronghold of my life"?

What is the psalmist confident that the Lord will do for him?

_____

_____

_____

_____

Does this mean nothing bad will ever happen to him? What does it mean?

_____

_____

_____

_____

Turn this psalm into a prayer, asking God to be these things for you.

Day 3

Read Psalm 63. Do you thirst for God? Or do you thirst for other things?

_____

_____

_____

_____

Why would a person thirst for God?

_____

_____

_____

Imagine being fully satisfied as with the richest of foods (verse 5). Can you imagine being that satisfied by God, whether or not your current outer circumstances change? Why or why not?

_____

_____

_____

Day 4

Read Psalm 91:1–8. Make a list of the images the psalmist uses to describe the Lord (shelter, refuge, etc.).

_____

_____

_____

Picture these things in your mind, and picture yourself finding safety there. Ask God to write one of these pictures on your heart to affirm the truth about who He is in your life.

Day 5

Read Psalm 91:1–8 again and then read verses 9–16 as well. The psalmist talks not just about the Lord but also about the kind of person the Lord protects. What does he say about this person in verses 9 and 14?

_____

_____

_____

_____

What does it mean to dwell in the shelter of the Most High (verses 1, 9)? How do you do this?

_____

_____

_____

_____

In practical terms, how do you make God your dwelling?

_____

_____

_____

_____

What does it mean to acknowledge God's name?

_____

_____

_____

_____

Ask God to show you what He wants from you. Thank Him that He doesn't ask for more right now than you can do right now. Tell Jesus that you trust Him.

TRUSTING IN GOD'S PROVISION

Consider It

In session 2, we read a story about a desperate widow crying out to a judge for justice. In this session, we will encounter another widow crying out for help. Widows appear frequently in the Bible because they were always among the most vulnerable in society. Few jobs were open to women in biblical times, so if a woman's husband died, she was often destitute. Men *did* die, sometimes when women had young children to look after, and a widow without family to care for her was in danger of starvation. It's no wonder, then, that widows represent us at our most needy and most dependent on God's provision to come through for us. We may not like to be in this position, but as we'll see in this session, God has reasons for allowing it.

1. *If you think of your life as a journey on foot through the mountains, how would you describe the portion of the path you are on right now? How rocky or smooth is it? How steep? Is it uphill, downhill, or level? How long has it been like this?*

Experience It

"I am leading you along the high road, but there are descents as well as ascents. In the distance you see snow-covered peaks glistening in brilliant sunlight. Your longing to reach those peaks is good, but you must not take shortcuts. Your assignment is to follow Me, allowing Me to direct your path. Let the heights beckon you onward, but stay close to Me. Learn to trust Me when things go 'wrong.' Disruptions to your routine highlight your dependence on Me. Trusting acceptance of trials brings blessings that *far outweigh them all*. Walk hand in hand with Me through this day. I have lovingly planned every inch of the way. Trust does not falter when the path becomes rocky and steep. Breathe deep draughts of My Presence, and hold tightly to My hand. Together we can make it!"

—FROM *JESUS CALLING*, JANUARY 18

2. *How do you usually deal with disruptions to your routine? What do these reactions indicate about your dependence on Jesus?*

3. *What does it mean to breathe deep draughts of Jesus' Presence and hold tightly to His hand? How does a person do that in practice?*

"You need Me every moment. Your awareness of your constant need for Me is your greatest strength. Your neediness, properly handled, is a link to My Presence. However, there are pitfalls that you must be on guard against: self-pity, self-preoccupation, giving up. Your inadequacy presents you with a continual choice—deep dependence on Me, or despair. The emptiness you feel within will be filled either with problems or with

My Presence. Make Me central in your consciousness by *praying continually*: simple, short prayers flowing out of the present moment. Use My Name liberally, to remind you of My Presence. *Keep on asking and you will receive, so that your gladness may be full and complete."*

—From *Jesus Calling*, February 22

4. *Why does God allow us to be in positions of neediness?*

5. *Describe what each of these would look like in your current situation: self-pity, self-preoccupation, giving up. What do their opposites look like?*

6. *What are some examples of simple, short prayers that flow out of the present moment?*

STUDY IT

Read aloud the following passage from 2 Kings 4:1–7. As you read this story from the life of the prophet Elisha, it will be helpful to know that olive oil was one of the most important staples in ancient Israel. It was essential for cooking, for medicine, and even for lighting homes, as the lamps the people used burned olive oil.

The wife of a man from the company of the prophets cried out to Elisha, "Your servant my husband is dead, and you know that he revered the LORD. But now his creditor is coming to take my two boys as his slaves."

Elisha replied to her, "How can I help you? Tell me, what do you have in your house?"

"Your servant has nothing there at all," she said, "except a small jar of olive oil."

Elisha said, "Go around and ask all your neighbors for empty jars. Don't ask for just a few. Then go inside and shut the door behind you and your sons. Pour oil into all the jars, and as each is filled, put it to one side."

She left him and shut the door behind her and her sons. They brought the jars to her and she kept pouring. When all the jars were full, she said to her son, "Bring me another one."

But he replied, "There is not a jar left." Then the oil stopped flowing.

She went and told the man of God, and he said, "Go, sell the oil and pay your debts. You and your sons can live on what is left."

During this time in Israel's history, creditors could enslave debtors and their children to work off a debt when they could not pay. Although God didn't do miracles like this every day, in this instance He chose to intervene in the situation through Elisha. In this way, he demonstrated to the people the kind of God He was and how He desired to take care of them. God may not do things so dramatically in our situation, but we can always rely on His provision and trust Him to take care of us.

7. *Spend five to ten minutes by yourself rereading the passage and picturing yourself in each scene. (The group leader will need to keep track of time.) You can put yourself in the place of the widow, or you can be in the room watching.*

Ask God to show you what He wants you to see in the passage. Use your senses to imagine the scene. What is the house like? What do you see? Hear? Smell? What do you feel when each person speaks? What tone of voice and body language does each person have? What do you feel as the oil is being poured? Write some notes about what you have recognized through this exercise.

_____

_____

_____

_____

_____

_____

_____

8. *When you sat in silence with this Scripture passage, how easy was it for you to imagine what was happening? How was this like or unlike the way you usually approach the Bible?*

_____

_____

_____

_____

9. *If you're meeting with a group, share your experience of putting yourself into the story of Elisha and the widow. What insights did you have?*

---

10. *This widow was completely dependent on whatever the Lord would provide to help her. How have you dealt with great neediness and dependence? What kinds of things do you do and feel when you are needy?*

---

11. *What goes through your mind when you think about crying out to God to meet your needs the way this widow cried out to the prophet Elisha? Does that seem to be the right thing to do? Do you experience any resistance to doing this?*

---

12. *What might God be impressing on your heart through this Scripture passage?*

13. *If you're meeting with a group, how can the group pray for you? If you're using this study on your own, what would you like to say to God right now?*

LIVE IT

The suggested Scripture readings this week deal with the theme of depending on God's provision to meet your deepest needs. Read the passage slowly, pausing to think about what is being said. Rather than approaching this as an assignment to complete, think of it as an opportunity to meet with a Person. Use any of the questions that are helpful.

Day 1

Read 2 Corinthians 12:7–10. According to verse 7, why was Paul given a thorn in his flesh?

According to verses 8–9, why didn't God take away the thorn when Paul asked Him to do so?

What does it mean that God's power is "made perfect" in every Christian's weakness?

Would you rather have God's power or your own? Why?

Pray for God to use the thorns in your life as ways to display His power.

Day 2

Read Psalm 56:1–4. This psalmist has enemies. In fact, many of the psalms speak of enemies, so this must be a theme worth thinking about. Who are your enemies? How do they attack you?

What do you need to trust God for regarding these enemies?

What are you afraid of?

_____

_____

_____

_____

Take your deepest fears to God and cry out to Him for safety. Complete this sentence: "Be merciful to me, my God, for _____. Provide for my needs." Picture yourself truly safe from your enemies. Tell God you trust Him.

Day 3

Read Ephesians 3:16–17. What does Paul pray for in verse 16? How would you restate that in your own words?

_____

_____

_____

_____

What could God's power in your inner being do for you?

_____

_____

_____

_____

How would it be helpful to have Christ dwelling in your heart through faith?

_____

_____

_____

_____

Turn these two verses into your own prayer, adding details about your situation. Tell Jesus you trust Him.

Day 4

Read Ephesians 3:17–19. What does Paul pray for? How would this be valuable for you?

_____

_____

_____

_____

What experience of the love of Christ have you already had?

_____

_____

_____

_____

In what ways do you need to know that love more than you do now?

Turn these verses into your own prayer, adding details about your situation.

Day 5

Read Ephesians 3:20–21. What does Paul say is true about God in verse 20?

Do you believe this? What helps you believe it?

What gets in the way?

_____

_____

_____

_____

What do you want to ask from God in light of these two verses?

_____

_____

_____

_____

Cry out to Him because of His unimaginable power, provision, and love. Tell Him you trust Him.

TRUSTING IN
GOD ALONE

CONSIDER IT

If we don't trust God to meet our needs, we have to trust someone or something else. It's impossible to get through the day trusting no one and nothing. If we mistrust others, we place our trust in ourselves and try to be as self-reliant as possible. Or if we doubt ourselves, we latch onto one or more other people. Or we become dependent on alcohol or binge on food or some other addiction that distracts us from a scary world. Many people trust a large and well-equipped military to protect their country, while others trust their own guns for protection. Some people trust money.

In this session we'll see why it is better to trust in God than any of these other things. Better than ourselves, better than other people, better than the finest military hardware.

1. *When your trust in God is shaky, who or what are you tempted to trust instead? Check as many responses as apply.*

___ Money	___ Myself
___ Police	___ Doctors
___ Friends or Family	___ Food
___ Work	___ Other (name it): _____

EXPERIENCE IT

"Refuse to worry! In this world there will always be something enticing you to worry. That is the nature of a fallen, fractured planet: Things are not as they should be. So the temptation to be anxious is constantly with you, trying to worm its way into your mind. The best defense is *continual communication with Me, richly seasoned with thanksgiving.* Awareness of My Presence fills your mind with Light and Peace, leaving no room for fear. This awareness lifts you up above your circumstances, enabling you to see problems from My perspective. Live close to Me! Together we can keep the wolves of worry at bay."

—FROM *JESUS CALLING*, MARCH 4

2. *In what ways does a person* refuse *to worry? What suggestions does this reading offer? What others can you think of?*

---

3. *Have you tried moving toward continual communication with God, richly seasoned with thanksgiving? If so, how is it going? If not, what do you think about trying it?*

"You have been on a long, uphill journey, and your energy is almost spent. Though you have faltered at times, you have not let go of My hand. I am pleased with your desire to stay close to Me. There is one thing, however, that displeases Me: your tendency to complain. You may talk to Me as much as you like about the difficulty of the path we are following. I understand better than anyone else the stresses and strains that have afflicted you. You can ventilate safely to Me, because talking with Me tempers your thoughts and helps you see things from My perspective.

"Complaining to others is another matter altogether. It opens the door to deadly sins such as self-pity and rage. Whenever you are tempted to grumble, come to Me and talk it out. As you open up to Me, I will put My thoughts in your mind and My song in your heart."

—From *Jesus Calling*, October 9

4. *How can you tell the difference between complaining and being open with the people close to you about your life?*

_____

_____

_____

_____

_____

5. *Why is it better to confide in God about the stresses you face rather than complain to others?*

_____

_____

_____

_____

_____

Study It

Read aloud the following passage from 2 Kings 6:8–23. This story, also from the life of the prophet Elisha, takes place in wartime, when horses and chariots were the most advanced military hardware of the day.

Now the king of Aram was at war with Israel. After conferring with his officers, he said, "I will set up my camp in such and such a place."

The man of God sent word to the king of Israel: "Beware of passing that place, because the Arameans are going down there." So the king of Israel checked on the place indicated by the man of God. Time and again Elisha warned the king, so that he was on his guard in such places.

This enraged the king of Aram. He summoned his officers and demanded of them, "Tell me! Which of us is on the side of the king of Israel?"

"None of us, my lord the king," said one of his officers, "but Elisha, the prophet who is in Israel, tells the king of Israel the very words you speak in your bedroom."

"Go, find out where he is," the king ordered, "so I can send men and capture him." The report came back: "He is in Dothan." Then he sent horses and chariots and a strong force there. They went by night and surrounded the city.

When the servant of the man of God got up and went out early the next morning, an army with horses and chariots had surrounded the city. "Oh no, my lord! What shall we do?" the servant asked.

"Don't be afraid," the prophet answered. "Those who are with us are more than those who are with them."

And Elisha prayed, "Open his eyes, LORD, so that he may see." Then the LORD opened the servant's eyes, and he looked and saw the hills full of horses and chariots of fire all around Elisha.

As the enemy came down toward him, Elisha prayed to the LORD, "Strike this army with blindness." So he struck them with blindness, as Elisha had asked.

Elisha told them, "This is not the road and this is not the city. Follow me, and I will lead you to the man you are looking for." And he led them to Samaria.

After they entered the city, Elisha said, "LORD, open the eyes of these men so they can see." Then the LORD opened their eyes and they looked, and there they were, inside Samaria.

When the king of Israel saw them, he asked Elisha, "Shall I kill them, my father? Shall I kill them?"

"Do not kill them," he answered. "Would you kill those you have captured with your own sword or bow? Set food and water before them so that they may eat and drink and then go back to their master." So he prepared a great feast for them, and after they had finished eating and drinking, he sent them away, and they returned to their master. So the bands from Aram stopped raiding Israel's territory.

6. *Spend five to ten minutes in silence rereading the passage and picturing yourself in each scene. (The group leader will need to keep track of time.) Concentrate especially on the events between Elisha and his servant, starting in the fifth paragraph. Put yourself in the place of the servant, and picture the scene. What do you see? Hear? Smell? What tone of voice and body language does each character use? What do you feel when the Lord opens your eyes? Write some notes about what you have recognized through this exercise.*

_____

_____

_____

_____

_____

_____

_____

7. *If you're meeting with a group, share your experience of putting yourself into the story of Elisha and his servant. What insights did you have?*

_____

_____

_____

_____

8. *What were the horses and chariots of fire? Why couldn't Elisha's servant see them at first?*

9. *Where do you see the themes of blindness and sight repeated in this story?*

10. *In every age, people are tempted to trust in advanced military hardware. Why didn't that work in this story?*

11. *What would have happened if Elisha had put his trust in himself? How is this lesson relevant today?*

_____

_____

_____

_____

12. *What might God be impressing on your heart through this Scripture passage?*

_____

_____

_____

_____

13. *If you're meeting with a group, how can the members pray for you? If you're using this study on your own, what would you like to say to God right now?*

_____

_____

_____

_____

LIVE IT

The Scripture readings for this week deal with the theme of trusting in God alone rather than the many appealing alternatives. Read the passage slowly, pausing to think about what is being said. Rather than approaching this as an assignment to complete, think of it as an opportunity to meet with a Person. Use any of the questions that are helpful.

Day 1

Read Isaiah 31:1–3. In this passage, Isaiah talks to those in his country who were placing their trust in a military alliance with Egypt. If you were to replace "horses" and "chariots" in this passage with something relevant to your life, what would it be?

According to verse 3, why is it foolish to trust in things or people?

How have you been let down by "horses and chariots"?

_____

_____

_____

_____

_____

Offer a prayer of trust to God, confessing to Him the other things you are tempted to trust.

Day 2

Read Psalm 20:1–6. Pray through this psalm slowly, stopping with each sentence to ask yourself how it applies to your situation. Adapt it to your circumstances.

> *Verse 1: "May the LORD answer you when you are in distress; may the name of the God of Jacob protect you."*

_____

_____

_____

_____

_____

Verse 2: "May he send you help from the sanctuary and grant you support from Zion."

Verse 3: "May he remember all your sacrifices and accept your burnt offerings."

Verse 4: "May he give you the desire of your heart and make all your plans succeed."

Verse 5: "May we shout for joy over your victory and lift up our banners in the name of our God. May the LORD grant all your requests."

Verse 6: "Now this I know: The LORD gives victory to his anointed."

Now read verses 7–9. Replace the chariots and horses with the things you are tempted to trust in other than God.

Verse 7: "Some trust in chariots and some in horses, but we trust in the name of the LORD our God."

Verse 8: "They are brought to their knees and fall, but we rise up and stand firm."

Verse 9: "LORD, give victory to the king! Answer us when we call!

Finish by praying, "I trust You, Jesus."

Day 3

Read Psalm 49:5–15. According to this psalm, in what things shouldn't we trust? What reasons does the psalmist offer for not placing our trust in these things?

Why do people so often trust in these things?

In verse 15, the psalmist says that God will redeem his soul "from the power of the grave" (NKJV). How does this represent the ultimate reason we should place our trust in the Lord?

Talk with God about your response to this psalm.

Day 4

Read Psalm 62:1–8. In verses 3–4, the psalmist talks about a problem he is facing. What does it seem to be?

The psalmist's solution is to "find rest" in God. What do you think this means? How is rest related to trust?

How does the psalmist describe God in verses 1–2 and 5–8? In what ways do you count on God to be your rock and fortress?

Pour out your heart to God, as verse 8 suggests.

Day 5

Read Psalm 62:9–12. In verse 9, the psalmist says social status is meaningless. In what ways has status—how important you are in other people's eyes— motivated you in the past?

Are you tempted to pursue status? If so, what would your life be like if it just didn't matter to you where you were in the pecking order?

_____

_____

_____

_____

Verses 11–12 say God is the source of power and unfailing love. In what areas of your life do you need those things?

_____

_____

_____

_____

Ask God to be your source today.

TRUSTING GOD'S GUIDANCE

CONSIDER IT

Sometimes we are going along with normal lives when something entirely unexpected occurs. A loved one has an accident. A job offer—or the loss of a job—changes our employment outlook. Or, as is the case in today's Bible passage, God directs our lives in an entirely different direction.

How do we respond to a sudden change of plans? Do we doubt and question God's guidance, or do we absorb the shock and step forward into the future with an attitude of complete dependence on Him? Sometimes we do a bit of both. In this session you'll have a chance to assess what you tend to do when the unexpected appears in your living room.

1. *What have been some of the major turning points in your life—the big life-altering ones such as marriage, pregnancy, job change, and health change? Name five events that stand out to you as the most significant.*

2. *Which, if any, of those major turning points were things you didn't plan? How did you deal with those unexpected ones?*

Experience It

"I am leading you, step by step, through your life. Hold My hand in trusting dependence, letting Me guide you through this day. Your future looks uncertain and feels flimsy—even precarious. That is how it should be. *Secret things belong to the Lord*, and future things are secret things. When you try to figure out the future, you are grasping at things that are Mine. This, like all forms of worry, is an act of rebellion: doubting My promises to care for you. Whenever you find yourself worrying about the future, repent and return to Me. I will show you the next step forward, and the one after that, and the one after that. Relax and enjoy the journey in My Presence, trusting Me to open up the way before you as you go."

—From *Jesus Calling*, February 26

3. *Does your future feel flimsy and even precarious at times? How do you normally cope when your life feels that way?*

4. *How does this reading recommend that you deal with your feelings about the future? What would that look like in practice for you?*

"Living in dependence on Me is a glorious adventure. Most people scurry around busily, trying to accomplish things through their own strength and ability. Some succeed enormously; others fail miserably. But both groups miss what life is meant to be: living and working in collaboration with Me. When you depend on Me continually, your whole perspective changes. You see miracles happening all around, while others see only natural occurrences and "coincidences." You begin each day with joyful expectation, watching to see what I will do. You accept weakness as a gift from Me, knowing that *My Power plugs in most readily to consecrated weakness.* You keep your plans tentative, knowing that My plans are far superior. *You consciously live, move, and have your being in Me,* desiring that I live in you. I in you, and you in Me. This is the intimate adventure I offer you."

—FROM *JESUS CALLING*, SEPTEMBER 2

5. *What attitudes would you connect to depending on Jesus continually and seeking His guidance?*

6. *Which of these attitudes are already normal for you? Which ones are not yet natural for you?*

7. How can you cultivate these less-natural attitudes?

_____

_____

_____

_____

Study It

Read aloud the following passage from Luke 1:26–38. In this story, an angel approaches a young woman named Mary and tells her she is going to be the mother of the Messiah. As you read, remember Mary was a teenager at the time—perhaps fifteen years old—and was living in a village in an obscure part of the world. Life was fragile for her people because they were ruled by the Roman Empire.

In the sixth month of Elizabeth's pregnancy, God sent the angel Gabriel to Nazareth, a town in Galilee, to a virgin pledged to be married to a man named Joseph, a descendant of David. The virgin's name was Mary. The angel went to her and said, "Greetings, you who are highly favored! The Lord is with you."

Mary was greatly troubled at his words and wondered what kind of greeting this might be. But the angel said to her, "Do not be afraid, Mary; you have found favor with God. You will conceive and give birth to a son, and you are to call him Jesus. He will be great and will be called the Son of the Most High. The Lord God will give him the throne of his father David, and he will reign over Jacob's descendants forever; his kingdom will never end."

"How will this be," Mary asked the angel, "since I am a virgin?"

The angel answered, "The Holy Spirit will come on you, and the power of the Most High will overshadow you. So the holy one to be born will be called the Son of God. Even Elizabeth your relative is going to have a child in her old age, and she who was said to be unable to conceive is in her sixth month. For no word from God will ever fail."

"I am the Lord's servant," Mary answered. "May your word to me be fulfilled." Then the angel left her.

8. *Spend five to ten minutes in silence rereading the passage and picturing yourself in the scene. (The group leader will need to keep track of time.) You can put yourself in the place of Mary, or you can be in the room watching. Ask God to show you what He wants you to see in the passage, and use your senses to imagine the scene. What do you see? Hear? How do you envision the angel? What tone of voice, facial expression, and body language does each character have when he or she speaks? What do you feel when each one speaks? Write some notes about what you have recognized through this exercise.*

9. *If you're meeting with a group, share your experience of putting yourself into the story of Mary and the angel Gabriel. What insights did you have?*

10. *Why do you think Mary was "greatly troubled" at Gabriel's greeting?*

11. *The angel said Mary was going to be pregnant without her fiancé's involvement. In her culture, pregnancy out of wedlock was a cataclysmic disgrace. It could easily have left her as an outcast, rejected by fiancé, family, and village. Yet Mary didn't meet Gabriel's announcement with a catalog of worries. Why do you think she was able to respond as she did?*

12. *What might God be impressing on your heart through this Scripture passage?*

_____

_____

_____

_____

_____

13. *If you're meeting with a group, how can the members pray for you? If you're using this study on your own, what would you like to say to God right now?*

_____

_____

_____

_____

_____

LIVE IT

The Scripture readings for this week deal with the theme of depending on God's guidance during times of change. Read the passage slowly, pausing to think about what is being said. Rather than approaching this as an assignment to complete, think of it as an opportunity to meet with a Person. Use any of the questions that are helpful.

Day 1

Read John 15:5 and Colossians 2:6–7. Ponder the image of Jesus as a vine and you as a branch of that vine, rooted in Him. What does this image tell you about how dependence on Jesus works? Why can you do nothing apart from Him?

_____

_____

_____

_____

How would consciously choosing to stay rooted in Him help you deal with a time of change?

_____

_____

_____

_____

How do you go about consciously choosing to stay rooted in Him? What practices does that involve?

_____

_____

_____

_____

Offer praise to Him as the vine you are rooted in, and ask Him to help you live in total dependence on Him as you face your current circumstances. Spend some time overflowing with thankfulness for making this possible.

Day 2

Read Jeremiah 17:5–8. According to verses 5–6, why is it disastrous to place your ultimate trust in people or yourself?

_____

_____

_____

_____

Picture a bush in the wastelands. Why is that an appropriate image for what the prophet is talking about?

_____

_____

_____

_____

What image does the prophet have of the person who trusts in the Lord (see verses 7–8)?

_____

_____

_____

_____

Picture yourself like that. What current circumstance do you need to approach in this way?

_____

_____

_____

_____

Ask God to help you trust in His guidance and to help you stay rooted in Him.

Day 3

Read Isaiah 40:30–31. Strength comes to those who "wait on" (NKJV) or "hope in" (NIV) the Lord. What does it mean to wait on or hope in God's guidance?

_____

_____

_____

_____

What does this involve in practice?

_____

_____

_____

_____

What are the benefits of doing this?

_____

_____

_____

_____

How can you build this into your life even more than you are now?

_____

_____

_____

_____

Take some time waiting on Him.

Day 4

Read Psalm 32:8–11. How do you think a person goes about paying attention to counsel from the Lord?

_____

_____

_____

How do you avoid needing a bit and bridle like a mule?

_____

_____

_____

Do you expect to get unfailing love (see verse 10) from the Lord? Why or why not?

_____

_____

_____

How has God treated you with unfailing love in the past? How is He treating you that way now?

Pray for the Lord's counsel and the ability to pay attention to Him when He gives it.

Day 5

Read Proverbs 16:3. What does the Lord promise to those who commit their ways to Him?

What does it mean to commit your ways to God? Is it a matter of asking Him to bless what you have decided to pursue? Is it a scheme for getting your own way? Where do trust and dependence fit in here?

How can committing your ways to the Lord help you in a time of change?

Commit your ways to the Lord right now, and see if you can carry that attitude with you throughout the day.

SESSION 7

TRUSTING IN GOD WHEN FACING THE UNKNOWN

CONSIDER IT

Failure. Nobody enjoys it. In fact, some of us hate it so much that we avoid trying things for fear of failure. But trusting God sometimes means trusting Him enough to step out of our comfort zone into the unknown, even the seemingly impossible. In that place, we're forced into radical dependence on Him. That's a good place for us to be, whether we succeed or fail. In this session, we'll explore one such step of trust.

1. *On a scale of 1 to 5, how would you rate your tendency to take risks and step out into the unknown?*

1	2	3	4	5
I avoid risk.				I love to take risks.

2. *Complete this sentence: "For me, my greatest fear in facing the unknown is*

_____."

EXPERIENCE IT

"You can achieve the victorious life through living in deep dependence on Me. People usually associate victory with success: not falling or stumbling, not making mistakes. But those who are successful in their own strength tend to go their own way, forgetting about Me. It is through problems and failure, weakness and neediness that you learn to rely on Me. True dependence is not simply asking Me to bless what you have decided to do. It is coming to Me with an open mind and heart, inviting Me to plant My desires within you. I may infuse within you a dream that seems far beyond your reach. You know that in yourself you cannot achieve such a goal. Thus begins your journey of profound reliance on Me. It is a faith-walk, taken one step at a time, leaning on Me as much as you need. This is not a path of continual success but of multiple failures. However, each failure is followed by a growth spurt, nourished by increased reliance on Me. Enjoy the blessedness of a victorious life, through deepening your dependence on Me."

—FROM *JESUS CALLING*, JANUARY 5

3. *What are the benefits of stepping into the unknown even if it results in failure?*

4. *Why is it best to ask the Lord to plant His desires in our hearts? Why might a person resist doing this?*

"Do everything in dependence on Me. The desire to act independently— apart from Me—springs from the root of pride. Self-sufficiency is subtle, insinuating its way into your thoughts and actions without your realizing it. But *apart from Me, you can do nothing*: that is, nothing of eternal value. My deepest desire for you is that you learn to depend on Me in every situation. I move heaven and earth to accomplish this purpose, but you must collaborate with Me in this training. Teaching you would be simple if I negated your free will or overwhelmed you with My Power. However, I love you too much to withdraw the godlike privilege I bestowed on you as My image-bearer. Use your freedom wisely, by relying on Me constantly. Thus you enjoy My Presence and My Peace."

—From *Jesus Calling*, September 6

5. *How might self-sufficiency sneak into a thought? Into an action? Give some examples.*

_____

_____

_____

_____

6. *If you found yourself sliding into self-sufficiency, how would you change your thoughts? Your actions?*

_____

_____

_____

_____

STUDY IT

Read aloud the following passage from Matthew 14:22–33. As you read, note that these events take place on the Sea of Galilee, a large freshwater lake in Israel about thirteen miles long and eight miles wide, surrounded by mountains. Jesus had just told His disciples to sail or row across the lake at night.

> Immediately Jesus made the disciples get into the boat and go on ahead of him to the other side, while he dismissed the crowd. After he had dismissed them, he went up on a mountainside by himself to pray. Later that night, he was there alone, and the boat was already a considerable distance from land, buffeted by the waves because the wind was against it.

Shortly before dawn Jesus went out to them, walking on the lake. When the disciples saw him walking on the lake, they were terrified. "It's a ghost," they said, and cried out in fear.

But Jesus immediately said to them: "Take courage! It is I. Don't be afraid."

"Lord, if it's you," Peter replied, "tell me to come to you on the water."

"Come," he said.

Then Peter got down out of the boat, walked on the water and came toward Jesus. But when he saw the wind, he was afraid and, beginning to sink, cried out, "Lord, save me!"

Immediately Jesus reached out his hand and caught him. "You of little faith," he said, "why did you doubt?"

And when they climbed into the boat, the wind died down. Then those who were in the boat worshiped him, saying, "Truly you are the Son of God."

7. *Spend five to ten minutes in silence rereading the passage and picturing yourself in the scene. You can put yourself in the place of Peter or one of Jesus' other disciples in the boat. Ask God to show you what He wants you to see in the passage, and use your senses to imagine the scene. What do you see? Hear? Smell? Feel physically? Feel emotionally? What tone of voice and body language does each character have? After five to ten minutes, write some notes about what you have experienced. The group leader will need to keep track of time.*

8. *If you're meeting with a group, share your experience of putting yourself into the story. What insights did you have?*

_____

_____

_____

_____

9. *What can we admire about Peter in this story?*

_____

_____

_____

_____

10. *What does this story say about depending on God in unknown situations? About experiencing failure?*

_____

_____

_____

_____

11. *What would getting out of the boat look like in your situation? What could encourage you to be braver about doing this?*

12. *What might God be saying to you through this Scripture passage?*

13. *If you're meeting with a group, how can the members pray for you? If you're using this study on your own, what would you like to say to God right now?*

LIVE IT

The Scripture readings for this week deal with the theme of trusting God enough to step into the unknown and try things. Read the passage slowly, pausing to think about what is being said. Rather than approaching this as an assignment to complete, think of it as an opportunity to meet with a Person. Use any of the questions that are helpful.

Day 1

Read Jeremiah 1:4–10. This is God's calling to Jeremiah to be a prophet. Why is Jeremiah's youth and inexperience irrelevant?

_____

_____

_____

_____

_____

What does God say when Jeremiah raises this objection?

_____

_____

_____

_____

_____

What promise does He make?

Spend some time in prayer today, asking God what He formed you to be and do. Don't worry if you don't get an immediate answer. It's enough to sit with the question and be open to whenever the Lord wants to show you.

Day 2

Read Psalm 18:27–29. Why do you think the Lord favors the humble over the haughty?

What does it mean for the Lord to keep your lamp burning?

Complete this sentence: "With the Lord I can _____." What does God want you to be brave enough to do in complete dependence on Him?

_____

_____

_____

_____

Ask Him for the strength and courage to do what He has placed on your heart.

Day 3

Read Psalm 18:30–36. What does this passage promise the Lord will do for those who trust in Him? List everything.

_____

_____

_____

For what battle(s) or unknown situations do you need this kind of help?

_____

_____

_____

_____

In what ways do you need strong "arms"? In what ways do you need stable "feet" on a level surface?

How, in practice, do you go about taking refuge in the Lord?

Turn this passage into a prayer for help in doing what the Lord has given you to do.

Day 4

Read Isaiah 12:2–6. Think about each item the speaker trusts the Lord to be in his life. How is each one important for you?

How important is God your salvation? Your strength? Your defense?

_____

_____

_____

If you were to make known to others the things God has done, what would you proclaim?

_____

_____

_____

When you think about doing that—making known the things He has done— does that scare you or excite you? Why?

_____

_____

_____

In prayer, offer yourself to be available to make His ways known.

Day 5

Read Joshua 2:1–13. Rahab risked her life to hide spies from the Lord's army. Why did she do that?

_____

_____

_____

_____

How did fear of the unknown move her toward the Lord rather than away from Him?

_____

_____

_____

_____

What kinds of fears would she face in siding with the Lord's army against the city where she had probably lived her whole life? What could she lose? What could she gain?

_____

_____

_____

_____

What is an area where the Lord is asking you to take a risk? How can you move toward the Lord in that situation rather than away from Him?

_____

_____

_____

_____

Ask Him to give you the courage to step out in faith.

TRUSTING IN GOD'S WILL

CONSIDER IT

Sometimes depending on God means *not* doing certain things. We don't worry. We don't complain. We don't rush around trying to get things done in our own strength. At other times, depending on God means acting in His will and *doing* certain things He has assigned to us. We aren't passive, but active. If the task looks big, depending on God requires a big step of faith. In this final session, we'll think about that big step of faith on the path of service that God lays out before His people.

1. *What is one thing about this study on trusting Christ that you are grateful for?*

_____

_____

_____

_____

2. *If you could give away to someone else one thing you've learned from this study, what would it be?*

_____

_____

_____

_____

Experience It

"Come to Me with your plans held in abeyance. *Worship Me in spirit and in truth*, allowing My Glory to permeate your entire being. Trust Me enough to let Me guide you through this day, accomplishing My purposes in My timing. Subordinate your myriad plans to My Master Plan. I am sovereign over every aspect of your life! The challenge continually before you is to trust Me and search for My way through each day. Do not blindly follow your habitual route, or you will miss what I have prepared for you. *As the heavens are higher than the earth, so are My ways higher than your ways and My thoughts than your thoughts.*"

—From *Jesus Calling*, May 18

3. *How easy is it for you to hold your plans lightly and set them aside when God has another idea? What encourages you to do this?*

4. *What helps you search for God's way through each day? Do you feel like you sense God's way, or is it still a mystery?*

"Trust Me enough to spend ample time with Me, pushing back the demands of the day. Refuse to feel guilty about something that is so pleasing to Me, the King of the universe. Because I am omnipotent, I am able to bend time and events in your favor. You will find that you can accomplish *more* in less time, after you have given yourself to Me in rich communion. Also, as you align yourself with My perspective, you can sort out what is important and what is not. Don't fall into the trap of being constantly on the go. Many, many things people do in My Name have no value in My kingdom. To avoid doing meaningless works, stay in continual communication with Me. *I will instruct you and teach you in the way you should go; I will counsel you with My eye upon you.*"

—From *Jesus Calling*, February 10

5. *What are some benefits of taking ample time with Jesus? What are the drawbacks of being constantly on the go?*

6. *Do you feel guilty or under pressure when you take ample time with Jesus each day? What motivates you to take the time?*

STUDY IT

Read aloud the following passage from Luke 9:10–17. In this story, Jesus feeds five thousand people with five loaves of bread and two fish. If this is a familiar story, try to put yourself into it as if you're seeing it for the first time.

When the apostles returned, they reported to Jesus what they had done. Then he took them with him and they withdrew by themselves to a town called Bethsaida, but the crowds learned about it and followed him. He welcomed them and spoke to them about the kingdom of God, and healed those who needed healing.

Late in the afternoon the Twelve came to him and said, "Send the crowd away so they can go to the surrounding villages and countryside and find food and lodging, because we are in a remote place here."

He replied, "You give them something to eat."

They answered, "We have only five loaves of bread and two fish—unless we go and buy food for all this crowd." (About five thousand men were there.)

But he said to his disciples, "Have them sit down in groups of about fifty each." The disciples did so, and everyone sat down. Taking the five loaves and the two fish and looking up to heaven, he gave thanks and broke them. Then he gave them to the disciples to distribute to the people. They all ate and were satisfied, and the disciples picked up twelve basketfuls of broken pieces that were left over.

7. *Spend five to ten minutes in silence rereading the passage and picturing yourself in the scene. (The group leader will need to keep track of time.) You can put yourself in the place of one of the disciples, either the ones who speak or the ones who watch the events. Ask God to show you what He wants you to see in the passage, and use your senses to imagine the scene. What do you see? Hear? Smell? What do you feel when Jesus speaks and acts? Write some notes about what you have recognized through this exercise.*

8. *If you're meeting with a group, share your experience of putting yourself into the story. What insights did you have?*

9. *In the third paragraph, Jesus says, "You give them something to eat." This is a moment when Jesus asked something of His disciples that tested their trust in and dependence on Him. What tone of voice and body language did you imagine in the disciples' response? How much trust do you think they had?*

10. *Has Jesus ever asked you to take action: "You give them something to eat"? If so, how did you respond? Were you inclined to say, "No, I can't"? Or, perhaps, "Yes, I will in my own strength"?*

_____

_____

_____

_____

11. *What does a truly trusting heart—a heart truly ready to follow God's will in any situation—say in those moments?*

_____

_____

_____

_____

12. *What might God be saying to you through this Scripture passage?*

_____

_____

_____

_____

13. *If you're meeting with a group, how can the members pray for you? If you're using this study on your own, what would you like to say to God right now?*

_____

_____

_____

_____

_____

LIVE IT

The Scripture readings for this week deal with the theme of depending on God to do what He has given you to do. Read the passage slowly, pausing to think about what is being said. Rather than approaching this as an assignment to complete, think of it as an opportunity to meet with a Person. Use any of the questions that are helpful.

Day 1

Read Luke 11:5–8. Like the story of the judge and the widow that you read several weeks ago, this story presents an outrageous picture of God. How is God like the friend who has locked up his house and gone to bed?

_____

_____

_____

_____

How is He different?

_____

_____

_____

_____

Verse 8 recommends that believers in Christ use "shameless audacity" (NIV) or "impudence" (ESV) or "persistence" (NKJV) in asking for things. Are you shamelessly audacious in prayer? What does that mean?

_____

_____

_____

_____

How does your current situation call for shameless audacity in prayer?

_____

_____

_____

_____

_____

Day 2

Read Luke 11:9–10. What is something you have been asking God to give you for a long time?

_____

_____

_____

_____

How do you feel about continuing to ask for it?

_____

_____

_____

How easy is it for you to keep knocking on a door that hasn't yet opened?

_____

_____

_____

Why do you think God would want you to do that?

Today, tell God about the things that have been on your heart for some time. Also pray with shameless audacity for the things God has given you to do.

Day 3

Read Luke 11:9–13. Think about your earthly father. If you asked him for a fish, would he give you a snake? If your answer is no, what lesson should you draw from this passage?

If your answer is yes, how will you ask God to help you see how He is different from your earthly father?

Trust is harder to build if you have had untrustworthy models as a child, but you can start anew today with your heavenly Father. Why do you think this passage emphasizes praying for the Holy Spirit?

_____

_____

_____

_____

For what do you need the Holy Spirit's help today?

_____

_____

_____

Day 4

Read Psalm 56:3–4. Why does the psalmist trust God?

_____

_____

_____

When you ask yourself the question, "What can mere mortals do to me?" what answer do you give?

As you think about doing what God has given you to do, do you fear what mortals can do to you? If so, what do you fear?

How is God stronger than those things?

Take your fears to God in prayer and ask for the Holy Spirit to strengthen you.

Day 5

Read Habakkuk 3:19. What does it mean to have feet like a deer's feet?

_____

_____

_____

_____

In what areas of your life do you need feet like these?

_____

_____

_____

_____

What are the heights God wants you to be able to walk on?

_____

_____

_____

_____

Offer Him a prayer of willingness to go wherever He takes you and a prayer of trust that He will provide you with deer's feet to tread there.

LEADER'S NOTES

Thank you for your willingness to lead a group through this *Jesus Calling* study. The rewards of being a leader are different from the rewards of participating, and we hope you find your own walk with Jesus deepened by this experience. In many ways, your group meeting will be structured like other Bible studies in which you've participated. You'll want to open in prayer, for example, and ask people to silence their phones. These leader's notes will focus on elements of the study that may be new to you.

CONSIDER IT

This first portion of the study functions as an icebreaker. It gets the group members thinking about the topic at hand by asking them to share things from their own experience. Some people may want to tell a long story in response to one of these questions, but the goal is to keep the answers brief. Ideally, you want everyone in the group to have a chance to respond to the *Consider It* questions, so you may want to explain up front that everyone needs to limit his or her answer to one minute.

With the rest of the study, it is generally not a good idea to have everyone answer every question—a free-flowing discussion is more desirable. But with the *Consider It* questions, you can go around the circle. Encourage shy people to share, but don't force them. Tell the group they should feel free to pass if they prefer not to answer one of these questions.

EXPERIENCE IT

This is the group's chance to talk about excerpts from the *Jesus Calling* devotional. You will need to monitor this discussion closely so that you have enough time for the Bible study. If the group has a long and rich discussion on one of the devotional excerpts, you may choose to skip the other one and move on to the Bible study. Don't feel obliged to cover every question if the discussion is fruitful. On the other hand, do move on if the group starts to ramble or gets off on a tangent.

STUDY IT

Try to do the *Study It* exercise in session 1 and in session 4 on your own before the group meets so that you can coach people on what to expect. Note that this section may be a little different from Bible studies your group has done in the past. In sessions 1–3, members will read the Bible passage, discuss the reading as a group, and then spend several minutes praying about what God wants to say to them personally through the passage. In sessions 4–8, members will spend five to ten minutes in silence first, before the main group discussion.

It will be up to you to keep track of the time and call people back to the discussion when the time is up. (There are some good phone apps for timers that play a gentle chime or other pleasant sound instead of a disruptive noise.) In sessions 1–3, members will spend only two minutes at a time in silence. In session 4, that time goes up to five minutes. By the time you get to session 5 and 6, they may be ready for ten minutes. Use your judgment based on feedback you get.

Don't be afraid to let people sit in silence. Group members can sit where they are in the circle, or if you have space, you can let them go off alone to another room. As you introduce the exercise, tell them where they are free to go. If your group meets in a home, ask the host before the meeting which rooms are available for use. Some people will be more comfortable in silence if they have a bit of space from others.

When the group gathers back together after the time of silence, invite them to share what they experienced. There are several questions provided in this study guide that you can ask. Note that it's not necessary to cover every question if the group has a good discussion going. Again, it's also not necessary to go around the circle and make everyone share.

Don't be concerned if the group members are quiet after the exercise and slow to share. People are often quiet when they are pulling together their ideas, and some of the exercises might have been a new experience for them. Just ask a question and let it hang in the air until someone shares. You can then say, "Thank you. What about others? What came to you when you sat with the passage?"

Some people may say they found it hard to quiet their minds enough to focus on the readings for the specified amount of time. Tell them that's okay. They are practicing a skill, and sometimes skills take time to learn. If they learn to sit quietly with God's Word in a group, they will become much more comfortable sitting with the Word on their own.

Remind them that spending time each day in God's Word is one of the most valuable things they can do for their spiritual lives. Also, imagining the Bible passage isn't the one right way to spend time with God. Analytical Bible study is also good, and they will be doing some of that in their daily Bible readings. This study simply exposes them to an approach they may want to add to their menu of ways to spend time with God in His Word.

One concern some people may have with the exercises that ask them to picture themselves in the passage is it requires them to "add" things to the text that aren't there. That's an important concern, but it shouldn't be taken to extremes. Whenever we read a story in the Bible, we have to imagine it to some degree in order to understand it. The question is whether we imagine it deeply or shallowly, deliberately or carelessly.

For instance, whenever we see someone speaking in the Bible, we need to deeply and deliberately imagine the tone of voice and body language with which the words are spoken. Is the speaker angry, afraid, joking? If the characters are on a boat in a storm, we need to imagine what it's like to be on a boat in a storm, or the story has no impact. Of course, our depiction of things like a character's tone of voice needs to be held lightly, because we could be wrong. But trying on the possibilities is something we're meant to do when exploring the text.

PREPARATION

It's not necessary for group members to prepare anything for the study ahead of time. At the end of each study are suggestions for ways they can spend time in God's Word during the next five days of the week. These daily times are optional but valuable, so encourage the group to do them. Also invite them to bring their questions and insights back to the group at your next meeting, especially if they had a breakthrough moment or if they didn't understand something.

As the leader, there are a few things you should do to prepare for each meeting:

- *Read through the session.* This will help you to become familiar with the content and know how to structure the discussion times.

- *Spend five to ten minutes doing the Bible reflection exercise on your own.* You'll be watching the clock when the group meets, so you'll probably have a more fulfilling time with the passage if you do the exercise ahead of time. You can then reread the passage again when the group meets. This way, you'll be sure to have the selected Scripture even more deeply in your mind than group members do.

- *Pray for your group.* Pray especially that God will help them learn to trust in Him in every situation they face.

- *Bring extra supplies to your meeting.* Group members should bring their own pens for writing notes, but it is a good idea to have extras available for those who forget. You may also want to bring paper and additional Bibles for those who forget to bring their study guides.

Below you will find suggested answers for some of the study questions. Note that in many cases there is no one right answer. Answers will vary, especially when the group members are sharing their personal experiences.

Session 1: Trusting in God's Strength

1. *Answers will vary. Use this opening question as a gauge to determine your group's overall perception of how they trust God.*

2. *Answers will vary. Because this is an entry into the topic at hand, it is important not to allow people's stories to go on and on. Again, if you have talkative group members, you may need to tell people to limit their answers to one minute.*

3. *Everyone has a tendency to get anxious at times. Sources of anxiety can include fears about a loved one, fears about an upcoming situation, fears of the unknown, and fears about change. Most of us worry when we feel we have no control over a situation or are anticipating loss.*

4. *Answers may include seeing sources of anxiety as growth opportunities to be embraced, letting go of regret, not thinking about what might have been, accepting things as they are, and leaning on Jesus.*

5. *Any of those same unfamiliar things may be appealing. Most of us want to be the way the reading describes, but it takes time to get there. However, some group members may have sources of anxiety that they don't want to embrace or things about their lives that they don't want to accept. It's fine for them to say so. It's a helpful first step for them to just acknowledge their areas of resistance.*

6. *One obstacle is a busy and distracted mind. You can suggest that group members post notes where they will see them or give themselves reminders in the calendar of their phones. Two or three reminders in a day can go a long way.*

7. *The benefits include seeing God more easily in situations, loosening the grip of fear on our lives, experiencing more gratitude, and having a stronger overall relationship with God.*

8. *Jesus says we do not need to worry because we are valuable to God. Just as He provides for the birds of the air and the flowers of the field, He will provide for our needs. Worry doesn't really accomplish anything—seeking God's kingdom is the real route to provision of daily needs. We can affect the present; we can't affect the future by worrying about it. Worrying about tomorrow takes energy away from today and detracts from what God wants us to do in the present moment.*

9. *Answers will vary. Some members may question whether the Lord really will provide for them. After all, there is so much obvious need in the world today. The point of the passage is we can't change anything by worrying about it; only trusting in God brings true security and freedom from worry.*

10. *Answers will vary. It's fine for this process to be unfamiliar at first. Again, be sure to keep track of time.*

11. *Answers will vary.*

12. *Some people may find silence intimidating at first. Anxiety can move us to fill the air with noise, but taking a moment to be silent before God is good for us. Let the members express their discomfort, but let it be balanced by those who found the silence strengthening. Helping people become comfortable with silence will serve their private daily times with God in wonderful ways.*

13. *Take as much time as you can to pray for each other. You might have someone write down the prayer requests so you can keep track of answers to prayer.*

Session 2: Trusting in God's Goodness

1. *Answers will vary. Remember to ask people to keep their answers brief, as some may want to talk at length about their week. The goal here is to get everyone thinking about how they trust God on a daily basis.*

2. *The "why or why not" is the important part here. We may get discouraged for many reasons, such as the fear that life will be unlivable without the thing we've asked for, or the fear that a lack of an answer means God doesn't care for us.*

3. *God is good and can do anything. His delays have a purpose: to train us. God wants to display His glory in our situations. Any of these reasons may motivate us to trust Him.*

4. *Answers will vary. Remember, every challenging situation we face provides us with an opportunity to deepen our trust in God.*

5. *Answers will vary, but we know we can trust God because the Bible says His character and His plans for us are good. Psalm 34:8 states, "Taste and see that the LORD is good; blessed is the one who takes refuge in him." In Jeremiah 29:11, God says, "I know the plans I have for you . . . plans to prosper you and not to harm you, plans to give you hope and a future."*

6. *Each person will imagine the judge differently, but the point is for them to imagine him vividly in some way so they can fully enter into the story Jesus is telling. In terms of the judge's attitude toward the widow, it is callous indifference. He doesn't care about her.*

7. *The judge is like God in that he holds the power of justice or injustice for the widow—he can grant what she longs for or refuse it. The judge is unlike God in that he doesn't care about the widow, whereas God does care about us (see 1 Peter 5:7).*

8. *Jesus' lesson is that if a horrible judge like the one in the story responds to persistence, a good judge like God will even more surely respond to persistence. God wants us to nag Him in prayer (see also Luke 11:5–8). He wants us to trust Him enough to persist in prayer and not give up.*

9. *The outrageous comparison is supposed to jar us into seeing that God is a far better judge than we often give Him credit for being. Jesus knows that in our heart of hearts, many of us see God as uncaring and indifferent to our suffering. He's big; we're small. Jesus wants to get at that belief and say that even if it were true, persistence would still be worthwhile. However, because God is indeed good, we have nothing to fear. More than that, Jesus wants to expose that belief to the light so that we'll see we're believing something unworthy of God.*

10. *Answers will vary. Some group members may admit they lack the widow's persistence or trust. Or they may say they have a need as strong as the widow's, so they should be passionately praying about it. Or perhaps some of your members have a similarly strong faith but simply don't know that God encourages and rewards such persistence.*

11. *Answers will vary.*

12. *Answers will vary.*

13. *Responses will vary.*

Session 3: Trusting in God's Presence

1. *Answers will vary. Note that these ratings are purely subjective, so one person's 5 may not be the same as another person's. The goal is to get the group members thinking about how they perceive their current situations.*

2. *Answers will vary. Keep the length of each person's response to one minute.*

3. *All of us at times can lose sight of Christ when we are wrapped up in a problem. Losing sight of Jesus usually leads to anger, fear, or deep sadness, as well as to actions aimed at coping with those negative feelings. Those actions may be constructive but are often destructive. If we maintain focus on Jesus, we may still feel anger, fear, or sadness, but the feelings are less overwhelming and our actions are less likely to be destructive.*

4. *A regular daily time with Jesus—scheduled—can be a great help. So can supportive friends who are also trying to build the same habit and who can check in with each other.*

5. *The unseen reality refers to all things eternal—God, heaven, the angels, and those believers who have gone before us to be with God. Encourage group members to talk about how they envision heaven, the realm of God. It's helpful for us to have more than a vague notion of heaven that seems unreal when set alongside our very real sufferings. Revelation 4 and 21 offer specific pictures of God's realm.*

6. *Some of your group members will find it easier to approach each day with gratitude than others. Remembering that God has promised to always be present with us (see Hebrews 13:5) and that He is guiding our steps can help us to accept what each day brings.*

7. *Answers will vary. Encourage those who are confident of God's Presence to talk about what it's like for them. Some will feel it, while others will know it but not as a feeling. This is a difference in temperament. It's not necessary to feel God's Presence to know He is there.*

8. *The treasure is the knowledge of God's glory, referred to in the previous verse. It is the experience of God's Presence. The jars of clay are our fragile bodies. Paul's point is that God's powerful glory (Presence) resides in fragile mortals like us so it's clear to everybody that the power comes from Him and not from us.*

9. *Paul describes his problems as pressing, perplexing, persecution-inducing, and able to strike him down. But as bad as they are, he can also describe them as light and momentary compared to the unseen glory he knows is waiting for him.*

11. *Answers will vary. Note that the time has been raised to three minutes each. You can decide if that seems like too much time, but don't be afraid of silence. God can work in people's hearts when they sit quietly in His presence.*

12. *Answers will vary.*

13. *Responses will vary.*

Session 4: Trusting in God's Provision

1. *Answers will vary. Again, because this is an icebreaker, make sure the group members do not tell long stories with details at this point.*

2. *Some of us are gracious about disruptions because we are more comfortable with being dependent creatures, while others of us get somewhat or very angry because we like to be in control.*

3. *To breathe deep draughts of Jesus' Presence means to cultivate awareness of Him, to revel in His Presence, and to choose to consciously depend on Him. To "hold tightly to His hand" is another way of describing that conscious choice to depend on Him—through prayer first of all.*

4. *God puts us in positions of neediness so we will turn toward His Presence and rely on Him as the source of our provision, rather than suffering the emptiness and despair of relying on ourselves or other "gods."*

5. *Answers will vary.*

6. *"Please help me, Jesus" and "I trust you, Jesus" are two examples.*

7. *Note that the* **Study It** *exercise in this session is different from those in sessions 1–3. Remember to go through it on your own before the group meets so you will know what to expect. Begin by reading aloud the introductory paragraphs in this section as well as the instructions for question 7. Then read aloud the Bible passage. As you introduce the exercise, remember to tell the members where they are free to go to work through the exercise.*

8. *Answers will vary. Remember the goal of this time is simply to expose the group to an approach for studying and reflecting on Scripture that they may want to add to their menu of ways to spend time with God.*

9. *Answers will vary.*

10. *Answers will vary.*

11. *Some may worry God will not answer them, or God will not choose to meet their need, or that the problem is not "big enough" to take to God. Others might have no problem in calling out to God like the widow did.*

12. *Answers will vary.*

13. *Responses will vary.*

Session 5: Trusting in God Alone

1. *Answers will vary. The goal here is to help group members identify what types of things or people they place their trust in instead of God.*

2. *We refuse to worry by choosing to set our minds on constant communication with God—living close to Him—and maintaining a grateful heart. There are other things we can do as well, such as confessing our worries to a friend and taking our thoughts captive.*

3. *Answers will vary. Encourage group members to pursue continual communication with God, for this will build their reliance on Him.*

4. *We can tell the difference between complaining and openness by listening to the words we speak and being aware of the emotions behind those words. What we say will either be filled with self-pity, denial, or anger, or will sound like a confession that acknowledges our weakness and neediness.*

5. *Confiding in God invites Him into our troubles and brings His thoughts into our minds, which leads to clearer perspective and even concrete solutions. It also puts God's "song" in our hearts—a settled attitude of joy and gratitude that can't be drowned out by circumstances. Complaining to others rarely leads to solutions or a more desirable state of mind.*

6. *Read aloud the introductory information before the question, along with the question itself and the Bible passage. Based on your feedback from session 4, you can decide whether to allow a longer period of silence this time.*

7. *Answers will vary.*

8. *The horses and chariots of fire were evidence of an army of angels. Because they operate within the spiritual realm, they normally go unseen by most people, though the prophet Elisha could see them because God enabled him to do so. Elisha's servant was blind to the Lord's army until the Lord opened his eyes in response to Elisha's prayer.*

9. *After Elisha prayed for God to open his servant's eyes, he prayed He would blind the soldiers of Aram—not just to the Lord's army but also to the physical world they could normally see. The soldiers were blinded until the Lord opened their eyes in Samaria, the capital city of Elisha's country. Everyone in this story is dependent on the Lord for what they can see, whether in the spiritual realm or in the physical realm. Sight is just one area of life where we are totally dependent on God, whether we know it or not.*

10. *Trusting in military hardware didn't work for the people in this story when the Lord exercised His power, which was far beyond any human strength. The people of God operate and succeed only by the might of the Lord.*

11. *Elisha would have been killed if he had trusted in himself. This story represents a dramatic case of that, but in reality we are always vulnerable whenever we stop trusting the Lord.*

12. *Answers will vary.*

13. *Responses will vary.*

Session 6: Trusting in God's Guidance

1. *Answers will vary. According to the Holmes and Rahe Stress Scale, the top ten situations that cause the greatest stress in people's live are: (10) retirement, (9) marital reconciliation, (8) dismissal from work, (7) marriage, (6) personal injury or illness, (5) death of a close family member, (4) imprisonment, (3) marital separation, (2) divorce, and (1) death of a spouse.*

2. *Answers will vary. Be sure not to place any judgment on people's handling of those surprises. Just let them briefly share what happened and how they reacted.*

3. *When the future feels flimsy and precarious, some of us will attempt to cope by worrying or panicking about our situation. Others of us will double down on efforts to try to control the future.*

4. *The best alternative to worry is to relax and enjoy the journey with Jesus. It is to hold His hand in trusting dependence, to keep turning to Him for guidance throughout the day, to deliberately turn away from frantic efforts to control things and people, and to confess to Him our tendencies for control and panic.*

5. *Attitudes connected to depending on Jesus and seeking His guidance include looking for the small miracles around us, beginning our days with joyful expectation, accepting weakness as a gift from God, keeping our plans tentative, and desiring to live and move in Jesus.*

6. *Answers will vary.*

7. *There are many ways to cultivate these "less-natural" attitudes, but each requires us to be deliberate about adopting them as part of a new mindset. We can (and should) also ask God to strengthen these attitudes within us.*

8. *Read aloud the introductory information before the question, along with the question itself and the Bible passage. Note that this Bible passage has frequently been depicted in artwork, so after group members have a chance to imagine it for themselves, you could share with them some ways artists have imagined it. Look up images for "Annunciation" on the Internet (this is usually what such paintings are called). Two famous (and very different paintings) of the Annunciation are by Fra Angelico and by Henry Ossawa Tanner.*

9. *Answers will vary.*

10. *We don't know what it was like for Mary to see an angel, but it would have shocked her. Even if Gabriel appeared to her as a man, she wasn't used to being alone with men other than family members, and his words of praise may have felt undeserved.*

11. *Mary believed Gabriel spoke for the Lord, and she trusted the Lord completely. Therefore, her lack of understanding and her inability to see the future weren't cause for worry. She knew she could depend on the Lord, even now that everything in her life had been turned upside down.*

12. *Answers will vary.*

13. *Responses will vary.*

Session 7: Trusting in God When Facing the Unknown

1. *Answers will vary. The purpose of the exercise is for group members to take an initial assessment of where they are when it comes to taking risks and stepping into the unknown.*

2. *Answers will vary.*

3. *Stepping out into the unknown—even when it results in failure—trains us to rely on God and never forget Him. We may grow spiritually more through our failures than our successes. Ultimately, the real victory is in spiritual growth.*

4. *We want the Lord to plant His desires in our hearts because His desires are for what truly matters. Our desires are often for lesser things, and while they may be* **good** *things, they are not always the* **best** *things. We may also fall into the trap of convincing ourselves that the things we want are more important or worthwhile than they really are. We resist God's desires when we doubt He knows what is best or when we believe that our happiness depends on having our desires met.*

5. *One way self-sufficiency might sneak into our thoughts is when we say to ourselves,* **God hasn't answered my prayers in this area, so I guess it's up to me to accomplish it.** *Self-sufficiency may sneak into our actions when we put in obsessively long hours to make something perfect without remembering God as we work or by not trusting in His call to rest. Or it might manifest as a burst of anger against someone who gets in the way of our goal.*

6. *Some ways to change an attitude of self-sufficiency are to offer up a prayer of dependence, seek God's forgiveness, apologize to anyone whose help we have snubbed, or take some time to rest.*

7. *Read aloud the introductory information before the question, along with the question itself and the Bible passage.*

8. *Answers will vary.*

9. *Peter was willing to take the risk of getting out of the boat. He had enough faith to do that, and initially he depended on Jesus to walk on the water.*

10. *Walking on water—or any endeavor that is beyond our self-sufficient power—takes total dependence on Jesus. Peter failed when he stopped relying on Jesus, but his failure wasn't the end of the world. Jesus rescued him so that Peter could try his next assignment from Jesus. Failure was an essential part of Peter's training process.*

11. *Answers will vary. Complete trust in God will always help us to be braver in any situation where we are stepping into the unknown.*

12. *Answers will vary.*

13. *Responses will vary.*

Session 8: Trusting in God's Will

1. *Answers for this final icebreaker will vary. Use this first question as a way for members to reflect on the most important principle they took away from the study.*

2. *Answers will vary.*

3. *We might be encouraged to set aside our own plans and embrace God's will for our lives if we find that course leads to less stress or greater victory, or if others around us have embraced God's will and found their lives are better because of it, or when clinging to our plans multiplies our confusion or our difficulties.*

4. *Answers will vary, but consistently seeking God's way will require retraining our minds to look to God before we dive into particular actions. The consequences we experience from failing to follow God's ways can also motivate us to seek Him first and help us develop this healthy pattern in our lives. Encourage your members who don't see growth in this area, as they may be growing more than they realize. If we're honest, God's way is always, ultimately, a mystery.*

5. *First, taking ample time with Jesus pleases Him. Second, we find that we can accomplish more in less time when we are grounded in Him. We have a clearer sense of what is important. We avoid busying ourselves with meaningless things, which is certainly a drawback of continually being on the go.*

6. *Things that get in the way of us seeking time with Christ might include pressure from inside us or demands from other people. We have to make hard choices about how to respond to those demands and learn what motivates us. An intimate relationship with Jesus—one spurred on by love for Him—will continually draw us toward Him.*

7. *Read aloud the introductory material as well as the Bible passage.*

8. *Answers will vary.*

9. *Answers will vary. Perhaps one or two of the disciples leaned toward Jesus, nodding their heads to show their willingness to trust Him in this moment. Others might have leaned away, shaking their heads in disbelief and looking at each other in their nervousness. The ones who speak are probably in the latter category—they don't believe Jesus can satisfy so many with so little food.*

10. *Answers will vary, but at some point in each of our lives God will call us to step out in faith and follow His will—apart from any talent or ability of our own.*

11. *A truly trusting heart says, "Yes, I will do my best with the strength and gifts You have given me, but I will depend on You from start to finish, leaving the results in Your hands. Please supply what I lack."*

12. *Answers will vary.*

13. *Responses will vary.*

ENJOY JESUS' PRESENCE.
FIND COMFORT
IN HIS PEACE.

FAVORITE QUOTATIONS *from* Jesus Calling

PEACE *in* HIS PRESENCE

Sarah Young

Selected quotes and scriptures from **Jesus Calling**
along with inspiring images will encourage you to
worship and find comfort in the peace of the Lord.

www.jesuscalling.com

THOMAS NELSON
Since 1798